YORK PERSONAL TUTORS

Film and Media

Martin J. Walker

Longman

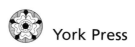
York Press

YORK PERSONAL TUTORS

titles in series

GCSE English

Novels and Short Stories
Shakespeare
Film and Media
Poetry
Drama
Spelling, Grammar and Punctuation

GCSE Maths

Number Book 1
Number Book 2
Shapes, Space and Measures
Algebra
Handling Data

YORK PRESS
322 Old Brompton Road, London SW5 9JH

PEARSON EDUCATION LIMITED
Edinburgh Gate, Harlow
Essex CM20 2JE, United Kingdom
Associated companies, branches and representatives throughout the world

First published 2000

ISBN 0582 40423-1

Designed by Shireen Nathoo Design, London
Illustrated by Spike Gerrell, Mike Perkins, Sholto Walker

York Press has endeavoured to seek permission and clear copyright on all illustrations and text produced in this Personal Tutor and given accreditation where necessary. In the event of any omissions, please contact York Press with any information which may be deemed appropriate for future editions. York Press would like to thank the following:
p.12 *Diehard* (1988) Gordon/Silver, Moviestore; *The Shining* (1980) Warner Brothers, Moviestore; *King Kong* (1933) RKO, The Kobal Collection; p.13 *Indiana Jones and the Last Crusade* (1989) Lucasfilm, Pictorial Press; *You Only Live Twice* (1967) Eon, Moviestore; p.14 *Psycho* (1960) Paramount, Moviestore; pp.15-17 *North by Northwest* (1959) MGM, The Ronald Grant Archive; pp.19-20 *No Way Out* (1987) Neufeld Ziskin Garland, Moviestore; p.27 *Metropolis* (1926) UFA (Erich Pommer), Ronald Grant Archive; p.29 *Invasion of the Body Snatchers* (1956) Allied Artists, Ronald Grant Archive; p.30 *Planet of the Apes* (1968) Upjack, Pictorial Press; p.33 *Forbidden Planet* (1956) MGM, Moviestore; pp.43-44 *Dracula* (1931) Universal, Ronald Grant Archive; p.45 *Halloween* (1978) Falcon, Ronald Grant Archive; p.47 Poster featuring Boris Karloff as *The Mummy* (1959) Universal, Pictorial Press; p.48 *Alien* (1979) Brandywine Shusett, Ronald Grant Archive; pp.57-65 thanks to *The Sun, The Daily Telegraph, The Mirror, The Independent, The Andover Midweek Advertiser, The Salisbury & Andover Avon Advertiser, The Bromley and Beckenham Leader, The Beckenham and Penge News Shopper, The West London Post, Bliss, Shout*; p.83 *Civilisation*, BBC, Ronald Grant Archive; p.86 Sean Bean in *Sharpe*; p.87 Helen Mirren in *Prime Suspect*; p.89 Advertisement for Pye Television (1953), Hulton Getty.

Typeset by Gem Graphics, Trenance, Mawgan Porth, Cornwall
Colour reproduction and film output by Spectrum Colour
Printed in Malaysia, VVP

CONTENTS

Introduction   4

A brief history of film   6

The thriller   10

Science fiction   26

Horror   40

Newspapers   56

Popular magazines   70

Television   78

Did you get it?   92

Index   96

INTRODUCTION

The National Curriculum
Media texts
Writing reviews

The National Curriculum requires you to develop the necessary skills to analyse, review and comment on media texts such as magazines, newspapers, television and films.

These skills are also requirements for GCSE English. Each of the different examination boards has its own interpretation of these requirements, though most examine the knowledge of media through coursework.

This book will take you through specific and clearly focused explorations of different media. We shall cover three different styles of film and explore newspapers, magazines and television. You will be able to use the book to guide you through media assignments for GCSE coursework.

Analysis of media texts

The problem with media such as film and television is that most people are so familiar with them that they rarely stop to think about how the media actually work. All that most of the audience would say about a film is that it is good or bad. This is not enough for a media assignment. You must analyse the elements that make a film good or bad. The same is true, in fact probably more so, for television. Because it is always there, little thought is given as to how and why certain types of programme reach the screen.

This book will help you to focus on aspects of writing, direction and production, and so look at media pieces as texts in much the same way that you would expect to look at plot and characters in a novel or play.

The book takes a practical approach. For instance, when you have learned how a storyboard is used, you will then be given the challenge of preparing one for your own film.

Journalists, film-makers and television producers working today all started somewhere. This book will help you to study media and to question and analyse what we see, hear and read.

You will develop the skills necessary for reviewing media texts effectively and maturely.

Reviewing media texts

Writing a review involves understanding what the film-makers or television producers were intending and examining the extent to which you think they have succeeded. The expression of personal taste alone does not constitute a review.

A BRIEF HISTORY OF FILM

Early days

The studio system

Fads and fashions

The world film industry came into being at the beginning of the twentieth century. Berlin and Paris were important centres for film-making and the industry was also developing in Britain. It was in America, however, that the production of films began to take place on a significant scale.

The American movie industry began in New York and this was the major centre for US films until 1912. A group of independent producers from New York went west to a suburb of the newly emerging city of Los Angeles. The suburb was called Hollywood.

Hollywood had distinct advantages over New York: particularly the favourable climate which allowed filming all year round. By the 1930s, with the advent of sound, Hollywood was the dominant film-making centre in the world.

For the first thirty years Hollywood operated under what was known as the 'studio system'. Small outfits quickly joined together to form large corporations. The 'Big Five' studios throughout The Golden Age of Hollywood were: MGM, Fox, Warner Brothers, RKO and Paramount.

The studio system made films on a production line basis. Actors, producers, directors and writers under exclusive contract to a studio could be assigned to whatever picture was being made at the time. This allowed new talent to be trained and gave the studio total control over its own pictures. Hollywood made hundreds of pictures a year ranging from short 'B movies' (used to support the main feature) to huge-scale epics.

THINK ABOUT IT

The studio system allowed movie executives total control over the output from the studios. This would suit movie executives, but not creative film makers.

In the 1940s, actors began to set up as independent film producers. The power of the studios was challenged. Now actors could appear in the films they wanted to it meant that each film had to start from scratch. Benefits of the studio system such as continuity and high production values were sometimes lost.

In the 1950s, the film industry began to lose audiences to the newly popular television. In an attempt to reverse the decline in attendance at movie theatres the industry began to use wide-screen. The first effective wide-screen process was *Cinemascope* owned by Fox, introduced in 1953. The other studios followed with their own versions such as *Warnerscope* and *Superscope*.

The process squeezed a wider picture onto standard 35mm film. When shown through the correct lens the picture was much wider than a normal film. The screen in the cinema had to be wider too. While the industry had some success with wide-screen it never regained the position it once held. Many directors disliked wide-screen because it distorted the shape of the picture. Samuel Goldwyn said, 'A wide screen makes a bad film twice as bad' whilst director Fritz Lang said, 'It is a formula for a funeral, or for snakes, but not for human beings'.

DID YOU KNOW?
Cinerama was the first of several fads aimed at getting people back to the cinema. Others soon followed, including Todd-AO, Cinemascope and 3D, but ultimately with little success.

By the 1980s, cinema attendances in Britain were in decline, reaching a low point of 54 million in 1984. The industry responded in a number of ways. Chief amongst these was probably the arrival of the multiplex cinema – the first of which appeared in Milton Keynes in 1985. Multiplex cinemas brought an improvement on the smoky fleapits of the past and catered for a wide audience in air-conditioned comfort. More screens meant that film producers could target a wider constituency than their original core market of 15–20 year olds.

This, in combination with blockbuster films, the first of which were Spielberg's *Jaws* (1975) and George Lucas's *Star Wars* (1977), caught the imagination of audiences and began to reverse the decline. In 1998, attendance had reached 140 million.

In addition to cinema audiences, film producers now sell their films through other channels such as video, cable and satellite TV, and DVD. The film industry is thriving once again.

NOTES

THE THRILLER

Elements

Characters

Case studies

The thriller is one of the most popular types of film. You can identify aspects of plot and character which are representative of the thriller. Thrillers range from courtroom dramas to complex capers involving crazed killers.

Alfred Hitchcock was a respected director closely associated with the development of the thriller. Hitchcock's plots were usually elaborate though the central reason for the actions of the characters was often rather vague. The plot was built around a device referred to by Hitchcock as 'The MacGuffin'.

The elements of the thriller

- **'The MacGuffin'** – is the reason the characters do what they do: searching for top-secret information or trying to cover up a past crime

- **Twists and turns** – devices used to keep the audiences guessing

- **Red herrings** – pieces of information which deliberately mislead the audience and possibly some of the film's characters

- **Big locations** – sequences shot in places such as the Statue of Liberty, Grand Central Station or Big Ben

A great chase sequence is often improved by having it take place in a grand setting.

- **Stock characters** – Part of the fun in watching a good thriller is trying to work out who the good guys are! Who is the hero and who is the villain?

- **Cliffhangers** – dramatic moments in the film when the hero appears to be in trouble

- **A trick ending** – a plot resolution that the audience didn't see coming.

KEY CONCEPTS

A thriller must be above all, thrilling ✳

All truly great thrillers have great final sequences ✳

Clues throughout the film point to the ending and to the identities of ✳
villain, victim and hero

N
O
T
E
S

Villain –Jack Nicholson as Jack Torrance in *The Shining* (1980)

Stock characters

There are essentially three character types in a thriller:

- The hero or heroine
- The villain
- The victim

Audiences can often make decisions about characters simply by the way that they look. Directors realise this and make use of it.

Victim – Fay Wray as Ann Durrow in *King Kong* (1933)

Hero – Bruce Willis as John McClane in *Diehard* (1988)

THINK ABOUT IT

Directors may develop tension either by keeping the audience uncertain about the identity of the villain or by letting the audience in on the secret — and enabling them to watch the hapless victim blunder about.

NOTES

The hero or heroine

This character can often be recognised immediately because a well-known actor has been cast in the part. Leading stars tend not to be killed off in the early stages of a film. Many stars play only hero or heroine characters. Take Harrison Ford as an example. No matter who is chasing him the audience knows that his character is not going to be killed. He will nearly be killed several times in order to create tension but he will survive and come to the rescue in the end.

Harrison Ford single-handedly outwits the Nazis in Indiana Jones and the Last Crusade (1989)

The hero or heroine figure is very often youthful, suave and sophisticated.

The villain

If the director wants the audience to be kept guessing then obvious villains must be avoided. Of course sometimes a director will deliberately make the villain behave stereotypically so that the audience do not believe it could be him or her.

A stereotypical villain is:

A shifty-looking Donald Pleasance in You Only Live Twice (1967)

- **Shifty looking** – perhaps with a particular mannerism that suggests he or she is unbalanced

- **Easy to spot in a crowd** – he would be the one dressed differently from everyone else.

In many thrillers however, directors conceal the true identity of the villain and so they might well be made to look and act like everyone else.

The Victim

It is never a good idea to be the partner of the good-looking cop or the room-mate of the beautiful girl! This is especially so if such a character is played by a leading star. If there is a crazed killer on the loose trying to kill the character played by a leading lady then the girl who is her room-mate is going to die. The leading lady usually survives but someone has to die just to show us that the killer means business. The good-looking cop usually has a partner who is a bit older than himself. The partner has a wife and seventeen beautiful children. If the good-looking cop gets invited to his partner's house for a family celebration then it is simply to build up audience sympathy for the partner the day before he gets killed. The good-looking cop will then spend the rest of the film avenging his partner's death.

THINK ABOUT IT

Building up sympathy for the victim and empathy with the actions of the hero is an important element of thrillers.

Janet Leigh as Marion Crane in the infamous
shower scene in *Psycho* (1960)

The thriller – two case studies

North by Northwest

Alfred Hitchcock
1959

North by Northwest *(Hitchcock, 1959)* displays all the elements of the thriller.

Roger Thornhill is escorted from the premises in
North by Northwest

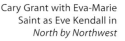

Cary Grant with Eva-Marie
Saint as Eve Kendall in
North by Northwest

The opening sequence of the film sets up the mistaken identity plot that is to run throughout. Hitchcock goes to great trouble to let us know that the character played by Cary Grant is called 'Roger Thornhill'. We see him being greeted by name in the foyer of his Manhattan offices and he is called 'Roger' by his secretary as she arranges his appointments. He arrives in a hotel lounge for a meeting but realises that he will be late going to his mother's house.

The order of events is crucial:

– A telegram boy enters the hotel lounge calling out that he has a telegram for a Mr George Caplin. The boy is watched closely by two men who look like they are up to no good.

– Roger Thornhill (Cary Grant) calls the telegram boy over so that he can send a message to his mother.

– The two men assume that Thornhill is calling the boy over in answer to the name George Caplin.

– The two men force Thornhill (who they think is Caplin) into a car at gunpoint and drive him away.

The audience knows that a mistake has been made. **Putting the audience ahead of the central character is a classic means of developing tension.** We know that Thornhill is innocent and who he claims to be, but we have to watch as he is taken for someone else.

THINK ABOUT IT

Why does Hitchcock go to great lengths to let the audience know the true identity of the character played by Cary Grant?

The villains are led by Mr Van Damme (played by James Mason). He is certain that he has captured Mr Caplin and orders him to be killed. A drunken Thornhill is put in a car and sent down a dangerous mountain road.

As Thornhill is a true thriller hero, he survives this attempt on his life. This is only the first of a series of 'cliffhangers' in the film. Cary Grant is going to survive no matter what happens.

Thornhill is mistakenly implicated in a murder at the United Nations building and has to go on the run. He boards a train where he meets the pretty girl of the movie, Eve Kendall (played by Eva-Marie Saint). She helps him to escape but is involved with Van Damme who is also on the train.

Roger Thornhill is attacked by a crop-dusting plane

Thornhill soon finds himself out in the middle of nowhere by a roadside on the American prairie. He thinks he is here to meet the real George Caplin and so end the mystery. Actually he has been set up by the girl and one of the most famous moments in cinema history follows as Thornhill is attacked by a crop dusting plane.

Several chase sequences later he finds out that Caplin never existed and was simply a decoy to put Van Damme off the scent of the real government agent who is right under his nose: none other than Eve Kendall.

The film reaches its climax on Mount Rushmore with a chase over the heads and down the faces of the American presidents carved into the mountain.

Most of the elements of the thriller can be found in this film:

– The villains are after some microfilm containing government secrets. We never find out what these secrets are – this is 'The MacGuffin'.

– The film has many twists and turns. Villains turn out to be good and good guys turn out to be villains. The only thing the audience really knows for sure is that Thornhill is a good guy.

– The film is full of red herrings, the best being that everyone is looking for George Caplin who doesn't exist.

– The film has big locations. Mount Rushmore and the United Nations building being two. These add to the impressive scale of the whole film.

– There are several notable cliffhangers in the film: Thornhill driving the car down the cliff-side road whilst drunk; the train being searched whilst he is on it; the attack by the crop-dusting plane and the actual cliffhanger on Mount Rushmore.

As an example of the thriller *North By Northwest* is hard to beat. Hitchcock's sly humour adds to the enjoyment of the film.

N
O
T
E
S

No Way Out

Roger Donaldson
1987

No Way Out *(Roger Donaldson, 1987)* is an example of how a thriller director can build essential tension.

George Dzundza, Kevin Costner and Will Patton consider the photograph in *No Way Out*

Kevin Costner stars as Lt. Tom Farrell. A girl with whom Farrell has been involved is murdered. Shortly before she was killed she had taken a polaroid picture of Farrell but the picture had come out blurred. Farrell was not the killer but the photo was found at the scene. No face can be recognised from the picture but a computer scientist has developed a new system for enhancing such images and is keen to try it out. The computer is working through most of the film, constantly getting closer and closer to revealing whose face was on the photograph.

Farrell has to find out who the real killer was, before the

Kevin Costner as Lt. Tom
Farrell in *No Way Out*

computer man arrives at a recognisable image. This one simple
plot device maintains tension for over an hour. It is a brilliant
use of time within a film and we know whose face will
eventually be revealed.

The audience has been put ahead of the central character.
The plot is complicated by the possibility that at least one of
the main characters is a spy. We do not expect this to be Farrell
as he has been built up to be the good guy. Throughout the
film the director makes the audience work hard to keep up and
to try to figure out who the hero really is. The tension is
maintained through the hunt for the real murderer and the
computer image generation that is taking place in the
background to the action.

The film obeys all the elements of the thriller and pushes
them to the limit with its use of bluff and double bluff. As far
as plot development goes this film has it all.

Now – build your own thriller

Now let's look at the way that a simple idea can be turned into a thriller with several possible endings.

Look at the following sketches which make up a storyboard for a thriller which may then have several possible endings.

1 A young man is seen in a restaurant, talking to a girl, Lisa.

2 Later he is found dead, killed by a pair of scissors in the back.

3 Lisa is seen in her office making an appointment with a client. She works for some sort of law firm perhaps – very respectable.

4 We meet the young couple of the film – David and Stephanie. They are engaged and are very excited about their new house.

5 Lisa is seen later that day following a man. She is obviously very interested in what he is doing but she doesn't approach him.

6 Later the same man is found dead, as before – scissors in the back.

7 David arrives for his appointment with Lisa. The camera is behind Lisa and we can see that she has a large pair of scissors in the desk drawer.

8 During the conversation that follows, Lisa drops something on the floor. As David reaches to pick it up he turns his back on Lisa. The camera zooms in on the scissors, now in Lisa's hand. Nothing happens.

The resolution

The film can now go in several directions:

– Lisa is the killer. She is a psychopath and perhaps she becomes infatuated with David, thus putting him in grave danger. Maybe Stephanie comes to the rescue – perhaps she is killed by Lisa.

– Stephanie is the real killer. She is mad and kills all her old boyfriends, so David is not safe and will soon be on her list. In this case Lisa needs a legitimate reason for meeting and following the victims – she is an investigator for a law firm which just happened to be handling the cases of both the dead men.

– David is the killer and is disposing of all of Stephanie's ex-boyfriends himself because he is insanely jealous.

– The killer is someone we have not met. This is rather weak and tends to annoy audiences who have spent two hours trying to figure out who the killer really is.

These are some possible ways in which this film could end. **Building in the opportunity for tricking the audience is important.** Don't forget that this format can work with a horror film (replace the psychopath with a monster) or a science fiction film (replace with an alien).

THINK ABOUT IT

Remember to keep up the tension. As soon as the audience knows everything, all suspense is lost.

Closing thoughts

Thrillers must make and keep the audience tense. Not with sudden shocks but with subtlety and cunning.

Music is often used to heighten tension in thrillers and give the audience subtle clues about the way the story is turning. Think about the menacing 'der-dum, der-dum' music in Steven Spielberg's 1975 film *Jaws* which hinted at the presence of the shark. The music created far more tension than the appearance of the somewhat rubbery creature at the end!

Look out for lingering shots of seemingly unimportant items. If the camera stays on a newspaper it is because you are supposed to read the report in it; if you see an address written down it is usually important.

The ending is always hinted at. It is up to the film-goer to pick up on clues and try to stay one step ahead. Information given in a throwaway manner might well turn out to be important.

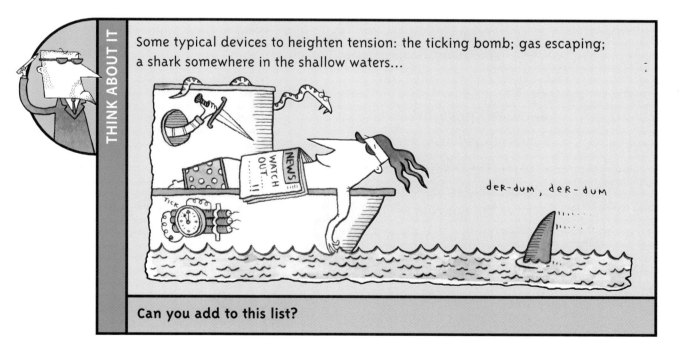

THINK ABOUT IT

Some typical devices to heighten tension: the ticking bomb; gas escaping; a shark somewhere in the shallow waters...

Can you add to this list?

HIGHER PERFORMANCE

1 Develop your own plot based around the idea of mistaken identity. Don't try to write a full script, write a synopsis instead. You might want to try some of the following:

- Make the central character seem innocent of the mistake surrounding his/her identity but later reveal that he/she knew all along what was going on.

- Choose suitable locations for key points in the film. You might want to use small scale everyday locations to bring a more gritty feel to the script.

- Decide on what it is that the bad guys want and whether or not they are going to get it. This is best done vaguely as the audience does not want to be bombarded with technical information as to what 'The MacGuffin' is.

- Think of a way to lead the audience to one ending and then surprise them with another.

2 Consider the following:

- A girl has witnessed a murder
- The killer saw her briefly
- He has tracked her down, but she does not know this
- He arrives at her house
- He gains entry to the house

Now storyboard the next sequence as we did on page 21.

Perhaps she hides successfully, maybe she attacks him or possibly he nearly gets to her when the doorbell rings and he is frightened away. The girl cannot be killed as she is a key part of the film's plot. You will probably use around ten storyboard sections.

Consider the types of shot that would be most effective in building up atmosphere in this sequence.

Quiz

1. What is *the MacGuffin* according to Hitchcock?

2. What is a red herring?

3. Define the term *trick ending*.

4. What do you understand by the term *stock characters*?

5. Why is a character often greeted several times by name early in the film?

6. Why might a director put the audience ahead of the characters?

7. What is meant by a *device* in a film?

8. Why does a director use a storyboard?

9. What is the MacGuffin in *No Way Out*?

10. Why is it not a good idea to be the close friend of the central character?

Answers

1. Whatever the spies etc. are after.
2. A deliberately misleading piece of information.
3. One that the audience did not see coming.
4. Typical characters such as the evil looking villain.
5. To establish the name of the character.
6. To develop tension.
7. A plot element as the crop dusting plane in *North by Northwest*.
8. Planning the camera shots.
9. The Polaroid photograph.
10. You are likely to die half way through the film just to give the hero a reason for revenge.

SCIENCE FICTION

Sci-fi as allegory

Sci-fi as a warning

Case studies

Science fiction films have two obvious elements: science and fiction. They are usually futuristic and often contain a view of how the world might be one day. They have also been used to show what is wrong with our own world by looking at the consequences of our actions.

Scientific advances have always fascinated and frightened mankind, from the invention of the crossbow to genetic engineering. Because we cannot really be sure of what may develop from our tinkerings with the natural world, film makers explore our fears by suggesting what may happen, good or bad.

Sci-fi – four case studies

Fritz lang
1926

Metropolis *(Fritz Lang, 1926)* was one of the first science fiction films and is famous for the huge scope of its production as well as for its nightmarish vision of the future.

The film is set in the year 2000 – this must have seemed a long way off in 1926! It was made at a time when some of the world's great cities were growing rapidly. With the recent arrival of electric light, the motor car and the aeroplane, many people believed that we would soon all be living in amazing space-age cities.

Fritz Lang explores what life might actually be like in such a city. The metropolis of the title is a mechanised city in which the people are enslaved by machines rather than served by them. A young girl, Maria, calms unrest amongst the people but a mad inventor creates an evil version of Maria to incite the people to revolution.

The film was shot on a huge scale with enormous geometric sets, and thousands of extras were used. It deals with unrest in society and is still relevant today because of the way it makes us think about modern life. It is as much about life in big cities in 1926 as it is a look into the future.

Metropolitan madness, *Metropolis*

Invasion of the
Body Snatchers

Don Siegel
1956

Invasion of the Body Snatchers *(Don Siegel, 1956)* is about a small American town invaded by creatures from outer space. The invaders steal the forms of the inhabitants. Large vegetable-like pods grow exact replicas of the townspeople. Once a copy has hatched it takes over the mind of the original person when they fall asleep.

Few people notice that this is taking place and when the hero does find out there is no-one to believe him. Many familiar ideas are found here, such as the man who is right but cannot get anyone to listen to him.

At the end of the film lorries are seen taking hundreds of pods out of the town to contaminate the rest of America.

This film works as an allegory: it represents something else. In 1950s America there was a great fear that the country would be invaded by communists. It was often thought that this invasion would come from within. Many people were accused of being communists and were investigated by the FBI. The notion that a set of ideas could spread like a disease is mirrored in the central idea of *Invasion of the Body Snatchers* with the taking over of people's minds being done slowly, quietly and secretly. America really did think that it was infected with communism and the film accurately reflects the paranoia felt at that time.

THINK ABOUT IT

Hollywood in the 1950s was bitterly divided by Senator Joseph McCarthy's efforts to uncover communism. The central idea is similar to that in Arthur Miller's *The Crucible* (1952)

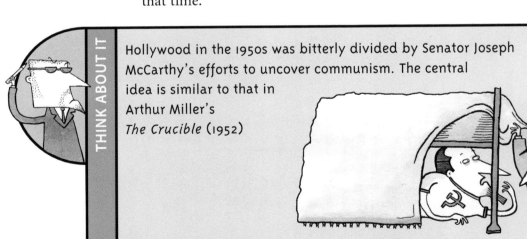

"INVASION OF THE BODY SNATCHERS" "X"

Starring

KEVIN McCARTHY · DANA WYNTER

AN ALLIED ARTISTS PICTURE

DISTRIBUTED BY ASSOCIATED BRITISH-PATHE LTD.

The body snatchers invade small-town America in *Invasion of the Body Snatchers*.

DID YOU KNOW?

Orson Welles panicked America in 1938 with his radio adaptation of *War of the Worlds*. It was performed as a series of mock news bulletins and was so convincing that millions believed they were being attacked by Martians.

Roddy McDowell as Cornelius in *Planet of the Apes*

**Planet of
the Apes**

Franklin
Schaffner
1968

Planet of the Apes *(Franklin Schaffner, 1968)* is a very good example of the way that science fiction can act as a warning to us that we must change our behaviour or pay the price.

Some astronauts, led by Commander George Taylor (Charlton Heston), land on a planet where apes rule and men are slaves. The apes have the ability to talk but the humans are mute. Their arrival means that the apes find out that man was able to speak at some point in his past.

The ape religion is called into question as it states that apes were created as divine and were the only creatures to be given a soul.

It is finally revealed that the planet on which the astronauts have landed is in fact Earth in our future. Mankind has all but destroyed the Earth and the apes have evolved to take charge.

N
O
T
E
S

The film draws on some well-known scientific ideas:

- Darwin's theory of evolution states that species adapt to suit their environments and that the strongest survive. When first published (and even today in some parts of the world) his theory caused uproar because it went against the word of the Bible.

- Today we can alter the genetic make-up of plants and animals. Some people believe that this is dangerous as we might produce monsters. In the film the humans of the future cannot speak. The film suggests that this has happened because of nuclear warfare and pollution.

- The argument about man having descended from apes is also examined in the film, though from exactly the other way round to the one we are used to. The suggestion is made that scientific knowledge which goes against current teachings might be kept secret.

THINK ABOUT IT

The suppression of dangerous ideas in the ape world mirrors the treatment of great scientists such as Galileo and Darwin.

Fred McLeod
Wilcox
1956

Forbidden Planet *(Fred McLeod Wilcox, 1956)* is a loose adaptation of William Shakespeare's *The Tempest* (1611), set in outer space.

A scientist has been stranded on a lonely planet with only his daughter for company. He has built himself a robot which can speak 187 languages and is able to make practically anything, including whisky!

A spaceship lands on the planet and before it can take off with the scientist and his daughter, members of the crew are killed by a mysterious monster which cannot be seen.

THINK ABOUT IT

Monsters are simply misunderstood like Dr. Frankenstein's unfairly maligned creation in Mary Shelley's *Frankenstein* (1818).

The scientist, Professor Morbius, has discovered a very advanced previous civilisation on the planet and has stumbled upon some of their secrets. He does not really want to leave this new knowledge behind, even when his life is in danger. In doing so, however, he has unleashed a monster from his own imagination. He learns that this is what had killed the former superbeings, the Krell: they were destroyed by their quest for too much knowledge.

The behaviour of Morbius is fairly typical of scientists in sci-fi films. They will sacrifice everything in order to look cleverer than other scientists. Any self-respecting scientist who discovered a new creature that is incapable of being killed and with a voracious appetite for human flesh would leave it on its planet and run away very quickly: not the scientist. The scientist wants to take it home, to study it and to teach it our ways. The trouble with scientists is that they don't watch enough sci-fi!

NOTES

Walter Pidgeon as Professor Morbius with Robby the Robot in *Forbidden Planet*

THINK ABOUT IT Morbius is obsessed with the search for knowledge and has allowed (and unwittingly brought about) the death of his fellow crew because of it.

Build your own sci-fi

As we've seen in this chapter, science fiction films are really quite formulaic. Have a go at creating your own science fiction film. Think about where you're going to set it (outer space, another planet, Planet Earth) and how your aliens attempt their takeover.

Have a look at the following plot and storyboard to give you some ideas.

Ships and aircraft have been mysteriously disappearing in the Bermuda Triangle for years, and nobody knows why.

1 Two marine biologists, one a young and handsome man, the other a feisty and attractive girl are studying sea life in the Bermuda Triangle on behalf of the US government. By chance, they pick up some strange transmissions from the sea bed.

2 Intrigued, they send down a miniature submarine to investigate.

3 The submarine bumps into a strange object on the sea floor. The two scientists are puzzled because it is like nothing they have seen before, and it is transmitting strange signals which jam electrical equipment.

4 Suddenly, earthquakes, volcanoes, tidal waves and high winds start to rip across the Earth's surface.

5 Satellites detect hundreds of extraterrestrial objects hurtling towards the Earth, and the US government transmits an SOS to their boat.

6 Our intrepid scientists realise that the extraterrestrial bodies are being summoned by the strange object, and that if they do not go down and destroy it, the Earth will be invaded.

N
O
T
E
S

7 The biologists dive down to the sea bed with a limpet mine full of high explosive, stick it on the object, and manage to retreat in time before the mine blows up the object.

8 Once this is destroyed, the extraterrestrial objects lose their way and retreat from Earth. Civilisation has been saved and the marine biologists fall in love.

So those are the bare bones of a plot and storyboard. But would cinema audiences be satisfied with such a simple storyline? Think about science fiction films you have seen recently. There is generally a sub plot that moves the scene away from the main plot, usually involving a baddie who is trying to make himself rich by exploiting the situation. Think of *Jurassic Park* (Steven Spielberg, 1993). The main plot involves the creation of a gigantic theme park of live dinosaurs brought back to life by DNA technology. The sub plot involves the fat computer operator who wants to make himself a fast buck by selling stolen dinosaur embryos to a rival biotech company. Of course his plans go wrong, and he is on the dinosaurs' lunch menu pretty quickly.

DID YOU KNOW?
In *Jurassic Park*, the attorney Gennaro was played by a computer-generated actor for the scene where he was eaten by the T-Rex. No live actors were harmed during the making of that scene.

What main subplot would you introduce into our Bermuda Triangle storyline? How about introducing a sinister captain on our scientists' boat who is an alien in human form sent to infiltrate our planet and make sure the transmitter summons the alien force. He has to be discovered somehow by our hero and heroine, and dispatched before the scientists can destroy the transmitter. How do they manage to do this?

You probably also enjoy films that have amazing special effects. Think of *Twister* (Jan de Bont, 1996) or *Men in Black* (Barry Sonnenfeld, 1997). What special effects might you commission for the Bermuda Triangle film? You will certainly need some dramatic computer animation of earthquakes, volcanoes and tidal waves. How about something a little less obvious, such as the alien transforming itself into the boat captain, or the transmitter producing some little transmitters that survive the explosion, just in time for the sequel!

You will be able to think of lots more subplots, twists, new creatures and technology. Film companies are always looking for new screenwriting talent. Why not have a go?

Closing thoughts

Science fiction films are predictable. Only the very good ones do anything other than discover an evil force in the universe and then spend the rest of the film being attacked by it, until the unlikely hero disables the fierce alien and brings about world peace.

In the 1950s the films were mainly American and often reflected the national paranoia over communism. Science fiction was seen as the stuff of B movies and big studios would not fund them. In the 1960s and 1970s science fiction films became more inventive and computerised special effects in the 1980s and 1990s produced films like *Jurassic Park* (1993).

THINK ABOUT IT

Remember, what might be obvious to us is rarely noticed by the crew of a spaceship.

Look out for stock characters:

- The scientist who will stop at nothing

- The brave young man destined to be eaten or zapped in the first twenty minutes

- The dim girl who goes looking for trouble

- The dashing hero who stops her from being eaten or zapped and finally saves the day

HIGHER PERFORMANCE

The notion of the quest for knowledge (irrespective of the costs) is one found frequently in science fiction films. Consider mankind's quest for knowledge and its consequences as a theme upon which to base the plot of your own science fiction film.

You will find it useful to read up on current controversial science stories in newspapers, and perhaps have a look at *New Scientist*, which presents contemporary science in a very readable way. Outline the scientific issue as simply and clearly as you can.

Now, choose your setting. If, for example you're basing your plot around the genetic modification of plants, and you want to make the vegetables mutate into carnivorous, mobile creatures, decide whether they have been grown in a laboratory, research centre, farm or even a garden, and who they will devour.

Decide who your villains, hero/heroine and victims will be, and draw up a cast list from your favourite actors.

Remember that you can be as wildly imaginative as you like with your storyline, but the best science fiction films are those which contain some scientific truths and unknowns.

Quiz

1. What are the two main elements of science fiction?

2. Which famous sci-fi film paralleled the fear of communism in America?

3. What word describes a story which can be interpreted on more than one level?

4. Name the Victorian scientist who changed world thinking with his famous theory of natural selection.

5. What warning does the ending of *Planet of the Apes* contain?

6. On which Shakespeare play is *Forbidden Planet* based?

7. In *Forbidden Planet*, what is the name of the previous inhabitants?

8. Which director made *Invasion of the Body Snatchers*?

9. Which successful trilogy made in the 1970s and 1980s has led to a further trilogy?

10. Which sci-fi character will stop at nothing to explore things?

Answers

1. Science and Fiction.
2. *Invasion of the Body Snatchers.*
3. Allegory.
4. Charles Darwin.
5. That mankind is likely to destroy itself.
6. *The Tempest.*
7. The Krell.
8. Don Siegel.
9. The *Star Wars* trilogy.
10. The scientist.

HORROR

Elements

Characters

Case studies

Horror films are hugely popular. From the early silent horror films such as *Dracula* and *Frankenstein,* audiences have lapped up the idea of terror. Apparently we all like to be terrified and will pay good money to be scared witless. Although there may seem to be many different types of horror film, they are all basically the same when examined carefully.

All horror films are essentially reworkings of the same story. One of the first major works is Bram Stoker's *Dracula* (1897). This novel contains the elements found in all horror movies. The monster might be called something different but the story is usually the same.

The novel uses Gothic settings. The Gothic period was actually from the twelfth to the sixteenth century and produced some of Europe's most famous cathedrals. When applied to literature or film, Gothic means something set in draughty old castles.

The horror movie itself has been part of the revival in modern cinema. Stars such as Jack Nicholson have broadened their appeal, and contributed to larger audiences.

The key elements of the horror movie are:

- A monster (without one you do not really have a horror film) which cannot easily be killed – handy for sequels

- There is always a group of stupid individuals, usually some variation on a couple, who couldn't recognise a monster if it bit them on the head

- Stupid people who go wandering about at night in draughty castles and big houses

- An expert who always turns up with information about killing the monster

- The minor characters are there to be eaten (preferably one of these will be a pretty girl, but a dim boyfriend will do)

- There will be a number of near misses with the monster before it is caught or killed

DID YOU KNOW?
Bela Lugosi uttered one of the most famous horror lines in *Dracula* (1930); 'Listen to them — children of the night! What music they make'.

Horror – four case studies

Dracula

Tod Browning
1931

Dracula *(Tod Browning, 1931)* concerns the young, ambitious Jonathan Harker who is sent to Transylvania to aid Count Dracula in purchasing property in England. When he gets to the castle he notices that Dracula appears only at night; he never seems to eat; there are no mirrors in the castle; many rooms are locked to him.

This worries him a bit, but of course he hasn't the benefit of having seen loads of Dracula films so he stays around. Dracula tells him to stay in certain parts of the castle for his own safety, so of course he goes wandering around in the parts that are off limits. In the course of so doing he is nearly dined upon by three vampire women: Dracula saves him at the last moment.

When Harker finally escapes from the castle, Dracula has set sail for England.

Back in Whitby, Harker's fiancée Mina and her friend Lucy are on holiday. They witness the arrival of a strange ship, blown impossibly into port during a freak storm. There is only one crew member aboard and he is dead and tied to the wheel. A large black dog is seen running up the steps to the ruined abbey. The ship's cargo is numerous large boxes.

Lucy starts to sleepwalk and appears pale each morning. It takes her friends ages to notice two puncture wounds in her neck and even then it requires the arrival of Professor Van Helsing to put the loss of blood together with the wounds. Her friends really are very dim.

THINK ABOUT IT

It seems to be a rule in horror films that most characters must be incredibly stupid!

He is not in time to save her, despite tons of wild garlic and strategically placed crucifixes. She dies – apparently. Actually she is now a vampire, one of the undead. The men, including her fiancé, Arthur, witness her wandering about the churchyard in her nightie and decide to kill her. Luckily for all concerned, the Professor has by now become an expert on vampires and how to do them in. He drives a stake through her heart and cuts off her head, which doesn't please Arthur too much.

The group of friends: Mina and Jonathan, Arthur, Van Helsing and two others set about finding the boxes Dracula brought to England as they now know, again very handily, that these contain earth from Transylvania which Dracula needs to sleep on. They just happen to be living above a lunatic asylum (very Victorian) and one of the lunatics has invited Dracula in to see him. This means the Count can now enter the house as he wishes (a vampire can only enter a house if he has been first invited).

Bela Lugosi as Count Dracula and Frances Dade as Lucy Weston in Dracula

Mina begins to look unwell, sleep badly and have terrible dreams. Do our friends see the similarities to Lucy? Of course not. They do not even notice the puncture wounds in her neck. She has now been infected and will turn into a vampire when she dies, unless Dracula is killed first. By now the men have found the boxes of earth so Dracula has to make a run for it.

A chase ensues as the heroes race to head off Dracula before he can return to his castle. They nearly catch him, then actually catch him and kill him. Mina is saved, as is the rest of the civilised world. Lucky really.

Bela Lugosi as Count Dracula and Helen Chandler as Mina Seward in *Dracula*

Halloween

John Carpenter
1978

Halloween *(John Carpenter, 1978)* features a crazed killer who escapes from a secure mental home where he has spent most of his life since murdering his family when still a child. Michael, the killer (and monster), is utterly without remorse and kills without reason. This makes him the most frightening killer of all as no one knows where he is going to strike. No one in the film that is. To the audience it is obvious.

Michael is going to pop up in the very house in which he killed his family. This is confirmed when the house turns out to be the one that Jamie Lee Curtis is to babysit in. Of course she

Don't go into the attic! *Halloween*

takes her boyfriend along. Generally speaking, the boyfriend of the major actress in the movie is there to be killed in a horrible way.

Whilst the two lovers are babysitting there is a noise outside. The boyfriend goes to investigate and is promptly murdered in a nasty way. Does the Jamie Lee Curtis character run out of the house when she finds he is dead and the 'phone is cut off? No, she runs upstairs into the room where Michael had killed his parents years before.

The psychiatrist who had been trying to treat Michael lends a hand for a while, thus providing the scientific interest. Several chases and trick endings follow and the killer disappears, presumed dead (until *Halloween 2* that is).

The film was described by critic Richard Combs as 'One of the cinema's most perfectly engineered devices for saying Boo!'

DID YOU KNOW?
America took nearly twenty years to catch on to the horror film. It was originally a German idea and many German film makers ended up in Hollywood because of it.

Poster featuring Boris Karloff as *The Mummy*

The Mummy
Terence Fisher
1959

The Mummy *(Terence Fisher, 1959)* and its sequels followed the same pattern. Archaeologists bring a mummy back to England, it wakes up and goes on the rampage. The scientists try to work out what is happening and some Egyptian mystic-types confuse everyone, including themselves.

The chase sequences are classic. The mummy walks very slowly yet always manages to catch its victims who, in reality, would have escaped with a nifty side step. This brings to light one more 'fact' about horror films which is that no matter how quickly the pursued character runs the monster always overtakes.

THINK ABOUT IT

If the victims could outrun the monster then the film would fall apart. After all how fast do you think a mummy with no internal organs could run?

Alien

Ridley Scott
1979

Alien *(Ridley Scott, 1979)* is essentially a horror film set in outer space. It has all of the stock horror movie characters:

- The whimpering girl
- The overly brave hero figure
- The stupid, greedy crew members
- The ambitious scientist (given a new twist here by making him an android)
- The monster that seemingly cannot be killed
- The resourceful girl who takes the monster on

Sigourney Weaver as Ripley with the ship's cat in *Alien*

This film is shot in a gothic spaceship. There is dripping water in dark corridors and jangling chains hanging from the ceiling. In spite of the fact that this is a ship capable of space flight there do not seem to be many lights on board. This has the effect of making the ship look like a candle-lit castle.

THINK ABOUT IT

No-one ever kills the monster when it is still a baby.

The scientist, who wants to study the alien, lets it on board. Once the monster has burst out of John Hurt's chest and is at large, people insist on wandering about the ship looking for it, sometimes one at a time. One even goes looking for the ship's cat – an obvious no-no.

The crew members are ripped apart and the handsome hero meets a nasty end after he goes to look for the alien in a small tunnel – as if you would. The whimpering girl is finally silenced in a particularly nasty way and the android ends up in bits. Only Ripley (played by Sigourney Weaver) can save the day.

The film has a trick ending, spiced up a bit by the fact that the ship is about to self-destruct.

Build your own horror film

The elements of the horror movie are really easy to define ▶ **see p 41.** Because of this the plot of a horror film is equally straightforward to set out. If you take a stereotypical example of the genre then you should be able to have a good deal of fun killing off dozy characters in nasty ways.

A scenario that always works well is this:

1 Newlyweds off on their honeymoon to a castle in the countryside. The car runs out of petrol on a desolate piece of road.

2 The only sign of life is a solitary light burning in the window of a creepy looking house in the distance.

3 The conversation that follows goes something like this:
"Gee Mandy, do you think they might have some petrol?"
"Oh I don't know Brad, it looks kind of spooky to me."

4 Having discussed the likelihood of being ripped limb from limb by the cellar dwelling psycho loony half-beast half-human son of the mad professor, our happy honeymooners head off to the house after all.

5 The front door is opened by an odd looking butler type who is obviously not all he seems – obvious to us that is.

6 Mandy and Brad are told to wait in the living room and not to go wandering off under any circumstances. Thirty seconds later Brad has gone wandering off.

7 It is now up to Mandy to find him.

From here the film can go in any direction that you want: you might come up with the sympathetic monster idea, e.g.

- Brad has stumbled into the cellar and been cornered by the beast who plans to pull him to pieces. Mandy hears the screams and finds the cellar. The beast is enchanted by her and lets them go.

- Brad might have to be sacrificed in order to develop the plot.

- Mandy cannot find Brad anywhere. She goes off to look for him in the part of the house that has been shut off for years. She opens the first door on the corridor – nothing. She opens the second door – crash – mop and bucket fall on her. The third door is slightly ajar. She opens it – and reveals Brad nailed to the wall with a nasty spike through his head.

You might want the creature to be killed by the girl or the rescuing hero yet to arrive on the scene. Perhaps the girl is killed and the bad guys win. There are only so many possibilities as far as endings go. Have fun applying them to the above scenario then work through some of your own. Ideas could include:

- The restless spirit that haunts a lonely house. The new owners begin to find out why their dream home was so reasonably priced

- The cute little girl in pigtails who is actually an evil witch. Lots of tinkly music and violent deaths

- Mysterious rituals in the old dungeon. People in funny robes messing about with sacrifices. The innocent group of friends that stumbles in on them is in big trouble

Once you have examined a few films of this genre you should not have any trouble in designing your own horror scenarios. Remember – horror films have monsters. Or do they?

DID YOU KNOW?
Although we've said all along that horror films have to have monsters, *The Blair Witch Project* (1999) has no obvious monster, no special effects, no blood or real shocks, yet it was one of the scariest films of the 1990s.

Closing thoughts

In recent years there has been something of a revival in horror film making. Two very successful films were *Scream* and *Scream 2*. In each case the film was full of references to the ways that horror films worked. the characters knew that certain things happened in horror films and openly discussed the plot. The films were one big "in joke" with the audience along for the ride. If you know the way that the horror movie works then it is very difficult to be frightened by the *Scream* films – though millions were.

Scream 2 is a 15 certificate and is a perfect illustration of plot and character in the horror film. Are you brave enough to watch it alone?

There are however many horror films on television in any one week. Try watching one and applying the criteria mentioned in this section.

HIGHER PERFORMANCE

1 Write your own horror film. Follow these simple steps and you too could be turning out terrifying scripts:

- Create a monster. You have two choices here: make the monster thoroughly evil or make it sad and lonely and not really murderous at all.

- Decide whether or not to give the creature a reason for doing what it does.

- Choose a suitably creepy setting: haunted house, old castle and so on.

- Select your victims. Couples whose cars break down are good for this. He always goes blundering off into the creepy house where he looks for help in – THE CELLAR. Inevitably he dies and she gets chased around a lot until the scientist and the hero arrive to save the day.

- Get a few good shocks in. Make the audience jump. The three door routine (see page 51) works well for this.

2 Write a review of a horror film that you have watched. Compare the film to the examples given in this book and be sure to point out the way that the film uses the elements of the genre.

Quiz

1. What does the term Gothic mean when used about film?

2. How are the vampires killed in *Dracula*?

3. What must a horror film have?

4. What are the two places that dimwits wander around in, in horror films?

5. What lies in store for the boyfriend of the leading actress?

6. What can be said of the victims in a horror film?

7. What is the three-door routine?

8. The creature in *Alien* seemingly cannot be killed. Why is this helpful?

9. How does the scientist in *Alien* conform to type (see chapter on sci-fi)?

10. What are the two basic types of monster?

Answers

1. Gothic settings such as old castles.
2. Stake through the heart and head cut off.
3. A monster.
4. Attics and cellars.
5. A nasty death.
6. They are usually stupid.
7. A device used to heighten tension.
8. Tension and possible sequels.
9. He studies the monster and does not kill it.
10. Thoroughly evil or rather lonely.

NEWSPAPERS

Layout

Content

Language

British newspapers fall loosely into two categories: tabloid and broadsheet. The word tabloid actually describes the size of the paper (half that of a broadsheet). Over the years the term tabloid has come to mean something in compressed form. Tabloid newspapers are quite different from broadsheets in style and content as well as in size.

Look on any newsstand and you will see the difference:

Tabloids		**Broadsheets**	
	The Express		*The Guardian*
	Daily Mail		*The Independent*
	The Sun		*The Daily Telegraph*
	The Mirror		*The Times*
	The Star		*The Financial Times*

THINK ABOUT IT

Many newspapers are part of media groups. In 1999 *The Times* and *The Sun* were both owned by News International. Should one organisation control this much news?

In this section, we will consider only the national daily
newspapers: local papers and the weekend papers include a
lot of extra material apart from news coverage.

If we take the most basic difference between broadsheet and
tabloid newspapers, it is the way they look.

Try this exercise. Buy two newspapers on the same day – a
tabloid and a broadsheet (such as *The Sun* and *The Guardian*).
Besides the obvious difference in physical size there will be
differences in the way that the front page is laid out.

THINK ABOUT IT

The front page of a newspaper is designed for
its target audience.
What assumptions is each newspaper
making about its readers?

N
O
T
E
S

The front page

Masthead
Contains the title of the newspaper and it's price

Headline
The lead into the main story

Advertisement
For an exclusive reader offer

Photograph

Text
The written element of the story

Byline
Tells you who wrote the story

Jump line
Takes you to the rest of the story

NOTES

If you look at the way any front page is put together, you will see that there are clear differences in style between tabloid and broadsheet. One way to compare the styles is in the form of a table. Fill in the table below with the percentages occupied by these devices in your newspapers.

% of Front Page	Tabloid	Broadsheet
Masthead		
Headline		
Text (Hard News)		
Text (Gossip)		
Photograph		
Graphic		
Adverts		

The balance of text and pictures will be quite different between your two papers. The general balance tends to be:

- **Tabloids** – a greater proportion of the page is given to masthead, headlines and pictures; coverage of a single story.

- **Broadsheet** – a greater proportion is given to text; coverage of several stories rather than one main story.

THINK ABOUT IT

Black and white photography is traditionally associated with news stories. Tabloids were the first to introduce colour photography. Its popularity quickly convinced the broadsheets to follow suit.

N O T E S

The role of the editor

Tabloids and broadsheets do not look different by accident. The language used in tabloids is simpler. The role of the editor is to establish a style and control the look of their newspaper according to their target readership.

Tabloid stories are generally shorter and punchier. If a tabloid journalist wrote a long, dense story, the editor would cut it. If a broadsheet journalist wrote a piece in the style of *The Sun*, the editor would not accept it.

DID YOU KNOW?

To give an idea of how many more tabloid than broadsheet newspapers are sold, look at these daily circulation figures from August 1999:

The Sun: 3,714,291

The Guardian: 392,617

It is the job of the editor, and the various sub-editors, to control how the paper looks and feels and then to include stories which suit the style.

The reason that daily newspapers look different is that each paper is trying to appeal to what it sees as its readership. The skill of the editorial team is to match the content and style of the paper to its readers.

It is too simple to say that the broadsheets use 'better English' or 'bigger words' than the tabloids. In fact the differences are far more subtle. The type of words used and the ways they are used vary from paper to paper.

Sunday papers differ from daily papers because the reader has more time to spend on the paper. So Sunday papers contain many more sections, including colour supplements which explore lifestyle issues, and specialist sections on travel, finance and job vacancies.

The Sunday Times was the first Sunday newspaper to introduce a colour supplement back in the early 1960s.

Editorial policy

The amount of *hard news* that a paper decides to print is determined by the editorial policy of the paper. Hard news is the type of story that has some substance to it. Major world events such as political stories and legal cases would fall into the definition of hard news. Tabloids feature political stories, though they prefer to focus on the personalities of the politicians rather than the actual issues.

There is likely to be a much closer correlation between the news in the broadsheets and the news on television. The lead story is often the same and the balance given to coverage of other stories is likely to be similar.

These stories, which are identified as important by both broadsheets and television, make up what we call the hard news of the day.

N
O
T
E
S

Pictures

Generally speaking, tabloids use more pictures than broadsheets. The total area of the paper given over to pictures is likely to be far greater in the tabloid – perhaps 25% as opposed to 10%. You can quickly estimate these figures for yourself.

Tabloid editors feel that their readers do not want lengthy and overly wordy coverage of events.

Tabloid stories are shorter and with more illustration than broadsheet.

THINK ABOUT IT

Local newspapers rely on sales in their home area. It pays them to mention as many local names as possible and to include as many photos as they can of neighbourhood events.

The tabloids tend to use pictures to liven up sensational stories: they are unlikely to have many photographs of politicians making speeches. One of the main differences between tabloid and broadsheet is this use of images. Both types of paper are good at choosing and displaying the images that they think their readers would like to see. Not only the tabloids use images effectively. Broadsheets often use striking photographs, though they are less likely to be covering celebrity scandal stories in the first place.

N
O
T
E
S

Language

Here are two front pages from the same day:

The headlines on the previous page show the basic differences between the two styles. An important story of the day before was that American bombers had been called back from a mission to bomb Iraq.

The Independent runs the story as the second lead item: 'Air strikes on hold as Baghdad concedes'.

The Sun relegates the story to pages eight and nine and the headline is: 'Blink and you're blitzed, Saddam'.

The two papers have taken a very different approach to exactly the same story. So, a major military conflict is considered to be much more important by one paper than the other.

The language used in *The Independent* is very different from that used in *The Sun*. *The Independent* uses language *objectively*. That means it reports the events without giving its own opinion. The key words 'Air strike', 'on hold' and 'concedes' are factual in nature.

In contrast, *The Sun* uses language *subjectively*. The style is more conversational in nature. Notice the tabloid's favourite trick – *alliteration*. Using 'blink' and 'blitzed' is typical. The headline is catchy and is clearly intended to stir up the reader. So the paper is advancing its view as well as reporting news. There is a threat contained in this headline. If the American president had used the exact words 'Blink and you're blitzed' then *The Sun* would simply be reporting a world event. But this is not the case, so the paper is putting its own slant on the news.

Using language subjectively is a common trait of the tabloid.

Emotive language is a feature found commonly in tabloids.

Tabloids rarely miss the opportunity to sensationalise any story.

Such features of language are to be found throughout the articles as well as in the headlines. Weighing up the balance between subjective and objective language is a useful way to look at the approach that a newspaper takes to news.

Of course not all stories in all newspapers are entirely serious. There are times when humour assists the telling of a story. It is for you to judge whether this is a good ploy to use on all occasions. Sometimes a story might be so serious as to preclude the use of a chatty style.

THINK ABOUT IT

The recent growth of free papers has begun to offer serious competition to local newspapers. Should we worry about this? After all, a free paper is only interested in the revenue it makes from taking advertisements, whilst a local paper documents the history of your home area.

Hard news vs gossip

To make possible a more detailed analysis of the two types of newspaper we must define what is meant by the term news. Broadly speaking 'news' can be divided into two areas: *hard news* which we discussed on page 61, and *gossip* which is self-evident.

The following exercise allows you to build a profile of the amount of hard news vs gossip that a newspaper carries. You need to:

- Watch or video the six o'clock or nine o'clock BBC news on one day
- Buy one tabloid and one broadsheet newspaper next day

You should select the top five stories from the newspapers and the TV news. The top stories in the papers can be identified by their placement (nearer the front page means more important) and the amount of page space they are given. The TV news stories are already ranked in order of importance by the broadcasters.

Now complete the following table by inserting 'hard news' or 'gossip' in the relevant spaces:

	TV News	Tabloid	Broadsheet
Story 1			
Story 2			
Story 3			
Story 4			
Story 5			

NOTES

Essay assignment

The keys to writing an essay are research and structure.

If you have completed the exercises given earlier in this chapter you should have a good deal of information from real newspapers. Careful planning will produce an essay which is logically structured and progresses sensibly from point to point.

If you were to produce an essay on the following theme, you could structure it like this, based on the work you have done on this chapter.

Say how you think British daily tabloid newspapers differ from broadsheets.

1   Brief general background to the two types of paper – explain the terms tabloid and broadsheet.

2   Look at the front page layout of each type of paper, text vs. pictures.

3   Discuss the language used by the two papers – subjective vs. objective.

4   Consider the amount of hard news that each paper carries – say what this tells you about the readership (or at least the editor's opinion of the readership).

5   Explore the way that each paper approaches a certain story – sensational vs. unbiased, straight reporting.

6   Give your thoughts on the two types of newspaper. Comment on the merits and disadvantages of each. Your personal opinion is very important here. You should support your comments with examples from real situations.

N
O
T
E
S

HIGHER PERFORMANCE

Write suitable broadsheet and tabloid headlines for each of the
following stories:

- Bank manager, Phil Fulton, caught stealing from the bank
- Speeding cyclist runs over roadsweeper
- Old lady wins lottery and gives millions to cats' home
- School choir wins trip to Berlin
- Giant plant found growing in English garden is totally
unknown, say scientists

Remember to make the tabloid headlines catchy, use alliteration
as well as slang words and expressions.
The broadsheet headlines must also grab the attention but
should be more serious in tone if the story is itself a serious
one.

Quiz

1. What aspect of a newspaper does the word *tabloid* actually describe?

2. Which type of newspaper sells the greatest number of copies per day?

3. What is contained in the *masthead* of a paper?

4. What does the *byline* tell you?

5. What does a *jump line* do?

6. How do papers give importance to stories?

7. Name the phrase that is often applied to serious news stories to differentiate them from gossip.

8. What is alliteration?

9. What is the point behind the use of *emotive* language?

10. Which person on the newspaper has the final say as to how it will look?

Answers

1. Its physical size.
2. The tabloid.
3. The title of the paper and the date, price etc.
4. Who wrote the story.
5. Takes you to another part of the paper.
6. By their placement.
7. Hard news.
8. The placing together of words which begin with the same sound.
9. To stir up the emotions.
10. The editor.

POPULAR MAGAZINES

The cover

Teen magazines

Case studies

There are hundreds of magazines published in Britain. They cover a wide range from specialist hobbies to general lifestyle issues.

One of the obvious differences between magazines and newspapers is the use of colour. Although daily newspapers use colour throughout it is not really their main feature. Magazines, however, are often printed on glossy paper to make the colours very vivid and attractive.

The cover

Popular magazines cover lifestyles, television, film and music. The covers make use of the following devices:

– Bright colours for background and text

– Large photograph of a model or television star

– Jump lines to tempting stories

– Perhaps a hint of scandal

– Fashion

The purpose of the cover is to persuade the potential reader to pick up the magazine and buy it. Covers often promise far more than they actually deliver inside.

Once inside, there are several elements that the reader can expect to find:

- **Feature articles** – These might be a glimpse into the life of a film star, a tour of his/her home, a review of the star's career to date. There might be an interview with the star. There will certainly be a good number of photographs to illustrate the story.

- **News and Gossip** – The chit-chat from the set of *EastEnders* or the latest developments in *Coronation Street* might appear in a television listings magazine. The idea of such material would be to keep the reader up-to-date with the comings and goings of favourite programmes, e.g. 'one legged banjo player to become new landlord of the Queen Vic – cast said to be hoppin' mad.'

- **Advice and letter pages** – These pages might simply feature reader's letters about personalities or letters to an agony aunt who replies to readers' concerns:

Dear Suzie,
My left arm is growing faster than my right. Is this normal and what should I do?

Dear Reader,
Wear your watch on your right hand otherwise you won't be able to reach it.

Teen magazines – two case studies

This area of study is very suitable for GCSE. The source material, i.e. teenage magazines is something that many of you are already familiar with. There is only one major problem with the area: **there are no magazines specifically aimed at teenage boys**

Magazines on football, computer games, minority sports all have large teenage male readerships but they are very different from the type of magazine that is aimed directly at the lifestyle of the teenage girl.

In the following case study we will be looking at teenage girls' magazines.

The teenage magazine market in Britain is huge with around a dozen top-selling titles at any one time. We will look at two in the following pages: *Shout* and *Bliss*.

Target readership

The front cover can tell you a great deal about the target readership of the magazine. Each magazine is fighting for its slot in the marketplace and needs to give out very clear signal to its potential readers. Seventeen-year-olds would not want to read about "my first kiss" any more than very adult issues could appear in a magazine aimed at twelve to thirteen-year-olds.

THINK ABOUT IT

If you want to sell a magazine to a fifteen-year-old-girl — put a glamorous eighteen-year-old girl on the cover. The publishers know that teenagers will fall for the "it's too old for you" trick and so buy the magazine. Few eighteen-year-old girls would be seen dead reading teen girl magazines — they are too busy reading adult women's magazines.

Cover styles

Shout uses colour very simply, has rather plain text and looks a little cluttered. The female models appear to be about twelve years old are wearing plain clothes and have young girls' hair styles – hair slide and hair band for example.

    Bliss is altogether more like a stylish woman's magazine – it even calls itself "The smart girl's guide to life". Colour is used very strikingly and the model appears older again, in fact she could easily be modelling for one of the adult female glossies (*Cosmopolitan*, *Red* etc). There is a more adult theme to the whole of the cover and the promise of an "11 page special report" on sex is boldly displayed in a banner across the whole cover.

NOTES

Contents

It is a good idea to compile a list of the contents of the magazines that you are studying. The relative amounts of fashion, gossip, celebrity news, true life stories and advice pages are what make each magazine different.

If you look at a magazine aimed at twelve-year-old girls you will probably find that it contains much the same as one aimed at the older teenager. It is often simply the tone that is different. If we look at different types of story from our two very different magazines, the contrasts should be clear.

Shout: readership girls 12+. Embarrassing moments are certainly embarrassing but quite innocent, e.g. 'I get embarrassed when my mum cheers my brother at football.' and 'I was sucking my pen in class when the ink went everywhere'.

Bliss: readership girls 15+. Many of the true life stories are sexual in nature – the publishers know sex sells magazines. Other typical features might be items such as 'Package brides' which deals with British girls on holiday being trapped into teen weddings.

Celebrity gossip

Shout: Typically these will be about boy bands or young female singers. The items will be short and deal with innocent aspects of the stars' lives, e.g. 'Mel C of the Spice Girls takes part in run for charity'.

Bliss: As well as the short gossip items dealing with who is going out with whom there tend to be longer items on particular stars, e.g. 'Is Ronan over Boyzone?' The feature might well involve a two or three page spread and go into more depth than would be found in the young girls' magazine.

Problems and advice

Shout: The problems were real enough but did not involve sexual matters. Typical items were problems such as 'My mate is being bullied' and 'The whole class turned against me'.

Bliss: In the magazines aimed at older girls the problem sections were headed: 'Love dilemmas, Life troubles, Sex queries, Body worries'. The problems were all quite adult in nature, many dealing with worries about sex and an obsession with body parts.

Language

The style of the language used changes according to the age of the target readership. The young girls' magazines use straightforward language and very basic vocabulary. The older girl's magazines imitate their adult counterparts and make greater use of 'in-words'.

Layout

The older the target readership the more sophisticated the page layout. Young girls do not seem to mind a very cluttered look – presumably the publishers think they have a short concentration span. There is a far greater use of striking colour and glossy paper in the magazines aimed at older girls. Here the publishers obviously think that the target readership wants to see something much more visually striking and mature.

HIGHER PERFORMANCE

1 Draft the outline of a new magazine. Make sure you have a definite target readership in mind. You should decide how many pages would be given over to celebrity news, fashion & beauty, real life stories, problems & advice, advertising.

2 Design a double page spread for each of the different types of pages that you intend to have. Pay particular attention to the use of colour and the style of language. (Do not simply cut out chunks from existing magazines.)

3 Write an accompanying explanation saying:

- Who the target readership is

- How you intend to appeal to the target audience

- Why you have decided on the particular balance of pages, percentage of fashion, gossip etc.

- How you have used colour and striking images to appeal to your readers

- Whether you feel you have been successful in your attempts

4 Conduct a survey among your friends and classmates to see what they thought of your ideas. You might well find that you have selected the right material for your readers.

Quiz

1. What is the name of the group of people the magazine is aimed at?

2. How do the models on teen magazine covers indicate the readership?

3. Which age range of magazine would use cheaper paper and simpler colour?

4. What is unusual about the teen magazine market?

5. Who would decide on the layout style of the magazine?

6. What types of story would you not find in a young teen magazine?

Answers

1. Target readership.
2. The female models are at least as old as the target readership.
3. Very young teenagers.
4. It is entirely female.
5. The editor.
6. Stories about adult issues.

TELEVISION

News

Entertainment and education

Sport and drama

News

One of the greatest differences between television channels is the way they present news. You might think that with the same information being available to each broadcaster the news would be the same on each station but as with newspapers there are different ways of presenting the same news.

DID YOU KNOW?
The longest established news broadcaster in the world is the BBC. It is generally regarded as being fair and objective. The BBC is not allowed to favour any one political party or point of view.

News plays a very important part in television schedules. In 1999 the decision to move *News at Ten* provoked much debate and it was even discussed in Parliament.

BBC news programmes follow a set pattern:

— Main headlines are given at the top of the news.

— Each story item is worked into a piece.

— The most important story leads, other stories are delivered in order of importance.

— The news ends with a weather forecast.

DID YOU KNOW?
This format has been widely used by other broadcasters too, in fact it was the only format for about thirty years on British television.

ITV news is often said to be tabloid in its nature. It treats some news stories the same way that a tabloid newspaper might, concentrating on the human interest.

Channel 4 News adopts a different format. This programme often spends in the region of twenty minutes developing one story. It does not go for the headlines followed by three minute story approach favoured by ITV and the BBC.

NOTES

Light entertainment

The term 'light entertainment' was first used by BBC Radio to distinguish popular entertainment from programmes such as opera or ballet. It comes in instantly recognisable forms:

The soap opera

Soap operas originated in America and were sponsored by soap powder companies who used them to sell soap to housewives in the advertisement breaks.

The BBC refused to produce or even show long running soap operas until the organisation realised that it was losing viewers in the mid evening slot.

EastEnders was the first home produced soap opera that the BBC showed. *Neighbours* followed soon after as the BBC began to fight for audience share with ITV.

Brookside was commissioned especially for the launch of Channel 4 and has been an important part of the station's scheduling ever since.

The spoof American show *Soap* was taken off television after complaints from moral majority types. It was a send up of the types of plot and character found in soaps. Apparently the outlandish plots of American soaps were allowed but satirising them was not.

The sitcom

Television companies just love the situation comedies. They provide big audiences for relatively little cost. Think of your favourite sitcom. It probably consists of a few characters who rarely leave the studio sets in which they live and work. There is no location filming. All filming is done in the studio.

The sketch show

For many years this has been the backbone of British light entertainment programming. Usually thirty minutes long, the show consists of short sketches and jokes to camera. From the sixties with shows such as *That Was the Week That Was* to the seventies with *Monty Python's Flying Circus,* and the eighties with *Not the Nine O'Clock News* through to *Spitting Image* with voices by Harry Enfield and then *The Fast Show* in the nineties, the sketch show has proved hugely popular.

The game show

Game shows are very popular. The host is usually a veteran comedian, assisted by glamorous hostesses. The game is simple enough for the average viewer to participate and the prizes can be quite lavish.

Educational programming

Pioneered by the BBC, and in fact for some time a condition built into commercial television franchise licences as well, the provision of educational programmes has been of major importance on British television. These fall in to two main categories: school programmes and 'distance learning' programmes, e.g. Open University programmes.

School programmes were broadcast during the day so that schools could watch them live (in the era before video recorders – yes there was one!). Now they are broadcast during the day in what is seen as slack time and in the middle of the night so that they can be recorded.

They are subject-based so that you get the school science programme, the school English programme etc. This has also opened up a valuable market in video sales. Schools can buy a complete series or perhaps performances of plays aimed directly at a school audience. Texts for examination are performed regularly on television.

Education found its way into children's TV with shows such as *Animal Magic, The Really Wild Show* and of course *Blue Peter*. Broadcasters perceive the young audience of today as the adult audience of tomorrow and have worked hard at building and maintaining loyalty through children's educational programmes. Commercial television was quick to grasp the fact that children could be persuaded to nag their parents for all sorts of artefacts once they had seen them on TV.

NOTES

Adult education programmes

Part of the BBC's charter to provide public service broadcasting includes adult education programmes. Popular among these are learning foreign languages, natural history and social sciences.

The Open University has broadcast on the BBC since the 1960s. Open University students can watch and record programmes that are integral to their courses. Such specialised material tends to be broadcast during the night.

Sir Kenneth Clark in the groundbreaking BBC educational series *Civilisation*

TV sport

The 1990s saw a major revolution take place in the broadcasting of sport on television. Until then the rights to televise major sporting events were held by either the BBC or ITV. If you wanted to watch Test cricket it was on the BBC, as simple as that. The FA Cup Final was often broadcast live by both ITV and the BBC as each saw it as a flagship event. With the advent of cable and Sky Television all of this changed.

DID YOU KNOW?
The first major sport to be bought up by Sky was Premier League football. It bought the rights when the Premiership was formed, though the BBC had the right to show highlights in *Match of the Day*. Soon to follow were:
England football internationals
Five Nations rugby
Test cricket (shared with Channel 4)
Several major golf championships

N
O
T
E
S

Formula One motor racing went from the BBC to ITV, though the BBC did manage to retain the rights to Wimbledon.

The governing bodies of major sports can now hold out to see who is the highest bidder and so attract the greatest sum of money possible for their sport. They would argue that this bring major benefits to sport – it certainly brings a good deal of money! When Sky TV and Channel 4 outbid the BBC for the rights to show Test cricket starting in summer 1999 there were complaints that the BBC had lost yet another sport that it had broadcast for years.

There is an argument for having certain sports on terrestrial television. Some people think that major events should not be owned by companies that restrict viewing to those who can afford to pay for it: after all, every household has already paid the licence fee.

As the televising of sport is a constantly changing thing it would be a good idea for you to compile an up-to-date list of major events and their broadcasters.

TV drama

Drama has long been a very important area of programme making. It generates huge sales revenue from abroad, with major dramas often being translated into many languages.

Costume drama

This is an area of programme-making where Britain is recognised as being the foremost producer in the world. Over the years most major writers have had their work dramatised.

The start of a new summer or winter season heralds the arrival of a new costume drama. The works of Jane Austen, Charles Dickens and the Brontë sisters are constantly updated for television. Because such drama serials demand period costumes they are referred to as costume dramas.

Sean Bean with his loyal band of troops in *Sharpe*

NOTES

Drama serials

What these serials have in common is powerful subject matter. The success of programmes such as *Prime Suspect* led to spin-offs – *Prime Suspect 2, Prime Suspect 3* and so on. Screening a story over a number of weeks enables the TV company to capture an audience – and improve their viewing figures.

Helen Mirren as Jane Tennant in *Prime Suspect*

THINK ABOUT IT

The police drama, such as *The Bill*, has its own rules of character, plot and setting. Its interest lies in a strong storyline and familiar characters.

The made-for-TV film

Film Four (Channel 4) and Screen Two (BBC 2) are two ventures that share the film-making costs between film companies and television production companies. The highly successful films *Four Weddings and a Funeral* (Mike Newell, 1993) and *The Full Monty* (Peter Cattaneo, 1997) were two such projects.

British films for television are few and far between because of the expense involved in making them. There are many more American TV movies though these tend to be low budget films that the Hollywood majors would simply not have touched.

N
O
T
E
S

TV advertising

Commercial television companies, both terrestrial and satellite, rely upon advertising revenue for programme-making and programme buying. Advertising is the only real source of revenue that commercial television companies have as they have no access to the licence fee.

Because of their reliance upon advertising, commercial television companies and the company advertising its product go to great lengths to ensure that the right adverts go out to the right viewers – their target audience.

The target audience is the single most important piece in the whole of the advertising jigsaw. If the various parties get the target audience wrong it could cost someone millions of pounds.

The advertising industry classifies each person according to wealth, occupation, education and social habits. The classifications are as follows.

A	Wealthy and educated	*high-flying business people, those who have made private fortunes etc*
B	Top grade professionals	*Lawyers, doctors etc.*
C	Other professionals	*Teachers, nurses etc.*
D	Skilled manual workers	*tradesmen e.g. plumbers, carpenters etc*
E	Unskilled workers	*factory assistants, labourers etc*

There are then the further sub-classes of 1 and 2, e.g. ABC 1, D2.

The most expensive group at which advertising is aimed is **ABC 1** as these people are able to afford luxury items such as expensive cars, exotic holidays and fancy gifts.

The next time you look at advertising on television try to work out what the target audience of the products actually is. If there are lots of advertisements for domestic products, you are probably watching a show that has a predominantly female CDE audience (the term sexism means nothing to advertisers); a flash car and boys' toys means the show is watched largely by ABC 1 males.

Advertisement for Pye Television from 1953

HIGHER PERFORMANCE

1 Try to account for the popularity of *Men Behaving Badly*.

2 To what extent you think that television is educational? Consider the roles played by news and current affairs programmes, documentaries, children's programmes, television drama.

3 "There is so little sport left on terrestrial television that the licence fee should be scrapped." What do you think?

4 Choose a television police drama and give a brief account of its characters, plots and setting. Explain its popularity.

5 Watch five different commercial TV programmes from different time slots in the week's television schedule. Make a note of every product advertised in the breaks before, during and after this programme (the video recorder would be useful here). Draw up your own chart of the programmes' viewer profiles according to the advertising industry classifications in the table. Write an account explaining the links you have observed between the programmes and the products advertised in them.

Quiz

6. Which university does the BBC have close broadcasting links with?

7. What TV revolution changed sport broadcasting in the UK?

1. When does the BBC broadcast its three main news programmes?

8. Which broadcasting corporation holds the rights for broadcasting Wimbledon?

2. What does the BBC news end with?

9. At the beginnings of which seasons are we most likely to see the arrival of a new costume drama on TV?

3. What type of programmes are regularly among the highest rated on TV?

10. What are Film Four and Screen Two?

4. Why are game shows so cheap to make?

5. Why were schools programmes originally broadcast during the day?

Answers

1. At one o'clock, six o'clock and nine o'clock.
2. The weather forecast.
3. Soaps.
4. There is only one star – the host – to be paid.
5. So that children could watch them at school.
6. The Open University
7. The advent of cable and satellite TV.
8. The BBC.
9. Summer and winter.
10. Ventures that share the film-making costs between TV and film production companies. Film Four is linked to Channel Four and Screen Two with BBC Two.

History of film

1 Which two cities were important centres for film-making at the beginning of the twentieth century?

2 Where did the American movie industry begin?

3 Where is Hollywood?

4 Why was Hollywood preferable to New York for film-making?

5 Which studios were known as the 'Big Five'?

6 Name two wide-screen processes.

7 What was happening to cinema attendances in Britain by the 1970s?

8 Where was Britain's first multiplex cinema built?

9 Name two blockbusters that helped attract audiences back to the cinema in Britain.

10 As well as the cinema, where do film producers sell their films?

Answers

1 Berlin and Paris.

2 New York.

3 In a suburb of Los Angeles.

4 The climate was more favourable.

5 MGM, Fox, Warner Brothers, RKO, Paramount.

6 Cinemascope, Warnerscope, Superscope.

7 They were declining.

8 Milton Keynes.

9 Jaws (1975), Star Wars (1977).

10 Video, cable and satellite TV, DVD…

Did you get it?

Film genres

1 Which director is closely associated with the development of the thriller?

2 Who plays the hero Roger Thornhill in *North by Northwest*?

3 How can music be effective in thrillers?

4 When was *Metropolis* made, and who was its director?

5 How are scientists usually portrayed in science fiction films?

6 Are sci-fi monsters really evil, or merely misunderstood?

7 What does Gothic mean, when applied to literature?

8 Who is the hero of the 1931 *Dracula* film?

9 In *Halloween*, Michael stalks which famous actress?

10 Which recent horror film has no obvious monsters?

Answers

1 Alfred Hitchcock.
2 Cary Grant.
3 It can help to build up tension, or make the audience jump!
4 1926, Fritz Lang.
5 Mad, determined to take over the world, or mess about with things they don't really understand.
6 Probably misunderstood, although they can appear pretty evil at times.
7 Gloomy, grotesque and supernatural.
8 Jonathan Harker.
9 Jamie Lee Curtis.
10 *The Blair Witch Project.*

Newspapers and magazines

1   Name three tabloid newspapers.

2   Name three broadsheet newspapers.

3   Why are weekend papers bulkier than weekday papers?

4   What is hard news?

5   How does a tabloid headline often differ from a broadsheet headline?

6   Name your three favourite magazines.

7   Who does *Shout* appeal to?

8   Who does *Bliss* appeal to?

9   What sort of magazines do eighteen-year-old girls usually read?

10 What does a magazine cover have to do?

Answers

1   *The Sun, The Mirror, The Express, The Daily Mail….*

2   *The Guardian, The Daily Telegraph, The Independent, The Financial Times…*

3   Because people have more time to read them.

4   Major world events, political issues, stories with gravitas.

5   Tabloid headlines are often jokey, emotive, or play on words. Broadsheet headlines are more serious and direct.

6   Whatever you like!

7   Girls 12+.

8   Girls 15+.

9   Young women's magazines.

10 Attract the reader and get him or her to buy the magazine.

Did you get it?

Television

1 Which news broadcaster has been established the longest?

2 The move of which TV news programme caused a debate in Parliament?

3 What is broadcast at the top of the news?

4 What does the news end with?

5 Name three TV soaps.

6 Why is TV drama an important source of revenue?

7 Account for the popularity of *The Bill*.

8 Do you think sport should be exclusively on cable and satellite TV?

9 If you were advertising a new model of BMW, which classifications of buyer would you aim it at?

10 If you were launching a new brand of bathroom cleaner, which classifications of buyer would you aim it at?

Answers

1 The BBC.
2 *News at Ten*.
3 The headlines.
4 The weather forecast.
5 *EastEnders, Coronation Street, Brookside, Neighbours…*
6 Drama series can be sold abroad to many countries.
7 It has strong storylines and characters, plot development and continuity, humour, drama…
8 It's up to you to decide.
9 AB1 males.
10 DE females.

Index

A
adult education 82, 83
advertising 88-9
Alien (Scott) 48-9
allegory in science fiction
    films 28-9
alliteration in newspapers 64
Animal Magic 82
audience
    advertising 88-9
    empathy 14
    sympathy 14
    tension 12, 16, 22, 23
    see also readership

B
BBC
    films for television 87
    licence fee 88
    news coverage 78-9
    Open University 82, 83
    sport 84-5
The Bill 87
The Blair Witch Project 52
Bliss 72-5
Blue Peter 82
Brookside 80
Browning, Tod 42-4

C
Carpenter, John 45-6
Channel 4 79, 87
characters
    horror films 41, 42, 46,
        50-2
    science fiction 37
    thrillers 11, 12-14
chase sequences 11, 17, 18
cliffhangers 11, 16, 18
communism, US 28-9
Costner, Kevin 19-20
costume drama 86
The Crucible (Miller) 28

D
Darwin's theory of evolution
    31
directors 12
Donaldson, Roger 19-20
Dracula (Browning) 41, 42-4
Dracula (Stoker) 40
drama on television 86-7

E
EastEnders 80
editors 60-1
educational programming
    82-3
empathy 14
essay writing 67

F
The Fast Show 81
Film Four 87
film industry 6-9, 87
Fisher, Terence 47
Forbidden Planet (Wilcox)
    32-3
Ford, Harrison 13
Four Weddings and a Funeral
    (Newell) 87
Fox 7, 8

Frankenstein (Shelley) 32, 40
The Full Monty (Cattaneo) 87

G
game shows 81
Goldwyn, Sam 8
gossip 66, 71, 74
Gothic settings 40
Grant, Cary 15-18

H
Halloween (Carpenter) 45-6
headlines, newspapers 64
hero/heroine 13
Heston, Charlton 30
Hitchcock, Alfred 10, 15-18
Hollywood 6-7
horror films 46
    Alien (Scott) 48-9
    The Blair Witch Project 52
    characters 41, 42, 46, 50-2
    Halloween (Carpenter) 45-6
    monsters 41, 47
    The Mummy (Fisher) 47
    plot 40-1, 49, 50-2
    Scream/Scream 2 53
    settings 40, 48-9
    storyboard 50-2
    vampires 42-4

I
The Independent 63-4
Invasion of the Body Snatchers
    (Siegel) 28-9
ITV news 79

J
Jaws (Spielberg) 9, 23
Jurassic Park (Spielberg) 35,
    37

L
Lang, Fritz 8, 26-7
language, written 60, 63-5,
    75
licence fee 88
light entertainment,
    television 80-1
locations 10, 18
Lucas, George 9
Lugosi, Bela 41, 43-4

M
McCarthy, Joseph 28-9
magazines
    advice and letter pages 71,
        75
    contents 74
    covers 70, 73
    feature articles 71
    language 75
    layout 75
    news and gossip 71, 74
    target readership 72-3, 74,
        75
media groups 56
media texts 5
Men in Black (Sonnenfeld) 36
Metropolis (Lang) 26-7
Miller, Arthur 28
mistaken identity 15-16

monsters in films 32-3, 41, 47
Monty Python's Flying Circus
    81
multiplex cinema 9
The Mummy (Fisher) 47
music for films 23

N
Neighbours 80
news coverage
    magazines 71, 74
    newspapers 61, 64-5, 66
    television 78-9
News International 56
newspapers 57, 61, 62, 65
    alliteration 64
    broadsheets 56-9, 60, 62,
        63, 66, 67
    circulation 60
    editors 60-1
    front page layout 57-9
    headlines 64
    language/target readership
        60, 63-5
    news coverage 61, 64-5, 66
    photographs 59, 62, 63
    tabloid 56-9, 60, 63-5, 66,
        67
No Way Out (Donaldson)
    19-20
North by Northwest
    (Hitchcock) 15-18
Not the Nine O'Clock News 81

O
Open University 82, 83

P
photography for newspapers
    59, 62, 63
Planet of the Apes (Schaffner)
    30-1
plot
    horror films 40-1
    science fiction 37
    and sub plot 35
    thriller 10, 11, 15-17, 18, 22
    trick endings 11, 49
Prime Suspect 87
production of films 7

R
radio drama, *War of the*
    Worlds 29
readership
    magazines 72-3, 74, 75
    newspapers 60, 63-5
The Really Wild Show 82

S
Schaffner, Franklin 30-1
science fiction films
    as allegory 28-9
    characters 37
    Forbidden Planet (Wilcox)
        32-3
    Invasion of the Body
        Snatchers (Siegel) 28-9
    Metropolis (Lang) 26-7
    monsters 32-3
    Planet of the Apes

    (Schaffner) 30-1
    plots 28-9, 30-1, 37
    special effects 36, 37
    storyboard 34-5
Scott, Ridley 48-9
Scream/Scream 2 53
Screen Two 87
Shelley, Mary 32, 40
Shout 72-5
Siegel, Don 28-9
sitcom 81
sketch show 81
Sky Television 84-5
Soap 80
soap operas 80
special effects, films 36, 37
Spielberg, Steven 9, 23, 35
Spitting Image 81
sport, television 84-5
Star Wars 9
stereotypes 13
Stoker, Bram 40
storyboards 21, 34-5, 50-2
studio system 7
sub plot 35-6
The Sun 63-4

T
television 84-5, 88-9
    advertising 88-9
    children's programmes 82
    drama 86-7
    educational programming
        82-3
    films made for 87
    licence fee 88
    light entertainment 80-1
    news coverage 78-9
    sport 84-5
tension 12, 16, 22, 23
That Was the Week That Was
    81
3D films 8
thriller
    characters 11, 12-14
    No Way Out (Donaldson)
        19-20
    North by Northwest
        (Hitchcock) 15-18
    plot 10-11, 20, 22
    storyboard 19
trick ending 11, 49
Twister (de Bont) 36

U
US
anti-communism 28-9
film industry 6-9

V
vampires 42-4
victims 14
villains 13, 14, 16, 18

W
War of the Worlds (Welles) 29
Welles, Orson 29
wide-screen 8
Wilcox, Fred McLeod 32-3